Anger and the Rocking Chair

An
Esalen
Book

Anger and the Rocking Chair

Gestalt Awareness
with Children

by Janet Lederman
Photographs by Lillian R. Cutler

McGraw-Hill Book Company
New York   St. Louis   San Francisco   Toronto

Library of Congress Catalog Card Number: 71–80971

First Edition
ISBN 07-036945-3
Design: Alan Peckolick

T his book by Janet Lederman is of extreme importance to the educational scene. It presents a vivid, clear and honest account of what can be done to provide real education for those who are usually not only neglected but affected in a powerfully negative way by an irritated educational system. Such students portrayed here by Janet Lederman obviously don't fit into the system. They are a source of irritation and sometimes provoke even stronger emotional reactions. That is why her class exists. Her methods, employing many principles of Gestalt Therapy, work with these students. For this accomplishment alone, an account of her teaching is of major relevance.

However, the importance of this book and the methods it so poetically describes does not stop here. What may be less obvious, but perhaps even more significant for the improvement of education in the classroom, is that what Janet Lederman does should be done by every teacher in every classroom, whatever the social class represented by the students, whatever the intelligence level or academic performance of these students.

Essentially, Janet Lederman attempts to increase an awareness of reality for each of her students. This includes a "finishing-up" of situations fraught with negative emotions, a "getting-in-touch" with the real self, its strengths and resources—as opposed to inadequate and distorted *concepts* of self—and a growing feeling of personal responsibility. Do not these goals seem appropriate for all students? I believe so.

Janet Lederman, in addition to her classroom teaching, is, at the time of this writing, a member of the staff of the Esalen-Ford project, committed to exploring ways to accomplishing these same goals without sacrificing basic content of the conventional curriculum. We in this project believe that approaches like the one described here will, in fact, strengthen conventional learning, both qualitatively and quantitatively. By skillfully translating the creative work of Dr. Frederick Perls, founder of Gestalt Therapy, into a classroom context, Janet Lederman has dramatically illustrated that these goals can be met.

Everyone connected with education in any way, formally or informally, should read this book at least three times.

George I. Brown
Graduate School of Education
University of California, Santa Barbara

This is a good book. It is a book of love and strength. It is a book of somebody who is in touch with herself and the world and thus can teach those children in despair how to get in touch with themselves and their world. In front of our eyes we see a miracle performed. We see what might be potential criminals find their bearings not in unbridled rage but in a center of a budding personality. We see the eyes of children opening to the possibility that they are somebody and not just a cauldron of desperate rage.

Janet Lederman is not control-mad. Thus, she is in control. Aware of her strength and unafraid, she teaches a flock of lost souls to find themselves and brings about a change from the anti-social to a socially valuable behavior. A beautiful start to heal some rifts in our torn society.

Frederick Perls, M.D., Ph.D.

To Fritz

The organism: interwoven; interlaced with pain and resentment. I see within this pain and resentment the energy . . . the potential for rebirth or for destruction. Yet, I also see that without waiting for the opportune rebirth of the organism, children ARE born.

I see children and also I see parents.

Parents, do you see your children? Do you see your child? Do you see a fragile and frightened child screaming for care and support? Or, surrounded by your own pain, do you experience only another pull, another tug . . . and the needing, needing, needing and begging for responses which you, yourself, are begging to receive?

I see teachers. I see teachers relating to children.

Teachers, do YOU see the child? Or do you see only your own image of what a child should be? Do you SEE his parents? Or do you SEE instead your own image of what parents are supposed to be and the skills you suppose them to possess? Do you dare to perceive your role as exciting, explosive, . . . innovative? Or, are you stuck in your impasse, fearful of your loss of tenure? Your loss of security? Content to strangle in comfortable apathy?

Parents and teachers, do you talk WITH each other?
Do you SEE each other?
Do you HEAR each other?

Or is your vision blinded . . . are your senses deafened?

Principals . . . Administrators . . . Boards of Education: Do you SEE and HEAR the people who look to you for leadership?

You say, there are too many people; there are too many problems; the system is too big; your hands are tied; . . . "The System," you say.

Mothers, you say you have too many children: you have so many problems; you have too much to do; there is no time to go to school. "I'd like to help . . . but . . ."

Teachers, you say there are too many children in the classroom. You can't teach "under those conditions." You were never really prepared for teaching in this "kind" of an area. It's a lost cause, you say. You have no more room to absorb the anger and resentment of the children, the parents. You say, no one really cares what you are doing, anyway. What did you say, Mother? No one seems to care about your child? The teacher can't control him? You say that the teacher lets him get away with "cussing." That it is up to the teacher to stop him, you say. Teachers, you can't teach. You can't stand trying to teach when six or seven children are always disrupting the room. Every time you try to discipline "the problems" you are met with "you're not my mother," and then you can't contact the parent. The principal won't do anything; he is afraid of community pressure?

The mother doesn't.
The teacher can't.
The principal won't.

You, sir. You say your wife speaks only Spanish and the school is not teaching your children enough. The children cannot read English and there is no one at home to help your children. You don't go to any of the parent meetings because you don't understand what is being said. You want to help your children . . . *but* . . .

Well, Mr. Principal . . . the district keeps sending you young teachers . . . fresh, unspoiled, just out of school. Young adults, inexperienced soon feeling inadequate and frustrated. The older teachers, you say, are worn out, worn down. You can't get extra classes or specialized personnel . . . it takes too long. It is too expensive. There are no funds. You say you're like a second lieutenant talking to a colonel. No one seems to understand the problems of *your* school.

A crowded urban community.
A meeting.
Parents and teachers, administrators, community leaders and workers. Those who do come add up to a mere handful, a hesitant, tentative group sitting in a large school auditorium. The leader (chosen by the Board of Education) begins by stating the need for communication. The few people who are gathered make awkward attempts to "communicate."

There is talk about homework.
There is talk about the P.T.A. meetings.
There is talk ... talk ... talk.

Words.

Parents, you try to say the words that will make you seem the "good parent."
Teachers, you try to say the words that will make you seem the "good teacher."
Principal, you try to say the words that will make you seem the "understanding principal."
Words ... words ... words.

Yet, each HAS an implicit common goal, a common goal which *must* be made recognizable. I say that the common goal *demands* to be made explicit.

CHILDREN.

"We want to educate our children!"
The organism suffocates as we are suffocating.
Educational institutions which do not release creative potential.
Limited specialized personnel
and everywhere fear ... fear ... fear.
Everywhere swallowed resentment.

The meeting continues. A teacher says to the parents . . .

> "I need your help. I want your help. I want your help in the classroom. I want us to be a team. I want you to see and to be a part of the problems I face. I don't want to hide from you!"

The parent responds . . .

> "I have babies at home. Sometimes I work. But I *want* to come to see the class . . . to help . . . to learn!"

Teacher . . .

> "Then let's join together . . . together let's find out what *we* want for our children. Hand in hand let's go to the Board of Education and demand what we want . . . what we need . . . what our children must have to grow!"

The principal enters into the exchange . . .

> "Good, we need parents, we welcome you. But . . . it is important that you be consistent. That you have a schedule to give us."

Ah, the veil . . . oh, so subtle . . . a partnership was about to occur . . . based on a common goal . . . a little trust had crept into the meeting . . . but now an impossible demand . . . an unreal expectation . . . a "consistent schedule."

Vision blinded . . . senses deafened

The principal who says . . . "You can if . . ."
The parent who now says, . . . "I would like to but . . ."

Frustration—
Excuses—

The conversation goes to . . .

"What about the parents who are not here?"
"How can we get them here?"

Now you no longer communicate with each other. Now you talk about the imaginary. You have lost contact with who IS available.

Vision blinded . . . senses deafened . . . resentment steeping.

I see that we are all inter-related . . . our lives tied together.
Yet, what is our fear?
What keeps us from seeing each other . . . frail . . . human . . . confused . . . AFRAID!

Vision blinded . . . senses deafened . . . resentment growing.

We deal with images . . .

> **with imagination**
> **with imaginary problems.**

We need to enter into the real "other" human being . . . NOT an *image* of

> **the teacher**
> **the poverty child**
> **the Spanish-speaking parent**
> **the administrator**
> **the black parent**
> **the white parent**

We need to open ourselves . . . to open our vision, to open our senses. We need to be aware of what IS and to relate with what IS.

I see each of us needing

> **to see himself**
> **to see his world**
> **to feel his relatedness**
> **to clear his vision**
> **to respond with his senses.**

I see you.
I hear you.

I sit in my rocking chair.
I see you.
Children with muscles taut;
bodies rigid;
frowns;
clenched fists.
I see your anger.
I sit in my rocking chair.
I am open,
flexing, moving,
strong.
I am comfortable and supportive.
I can be used by you.
I sit in my rocking chair.

Children, you can yell at this rocking chair. You can kick it.
Soon some of you will yell at me; some of you will kick me; some of
you will bite me or will hit me. I will spank you. I may even
wrestle with you. Then, little child, you will put up such a fight!
You will fight with every bit of anger you have, and I will fight you
back. Our bodies will touch. You will experience my strength.
You will be in touch with my willingness to be in touch with your
anger. I am not afraid of your reality. You will try to get away. I may
even have to sit on you and then you will let your tears flow . . . a
"bully," beginning to melt into childhood. Your taut muscles begin to
relax; your sobs begin to fade. I get off. I am not holding you down
anymore. If you want to go, I will not stop you now. You don't
run away. You are quiet and we are side by side.

"What did you do, Mark?"

"I bit you."

"What did I do when you bit me?"

"You spanked me."

I take your hand. You let me. You do not pull away. Together we walk over to the rocking chair. You sit on my lap. We talk. We hug. I pet you. You feel good to me. You are a child. I am an adult. I give you a cloth to wipe the perspiration from your face.

"What do you want to do now, Mark?"

"I don't know."

"I have an idea. See if you like it." You are very quiet now. "You could sit in the rocking chair and just rock for awhile."

We get up. You climb back into the rocking chair. You put your thumb in your mouth and you rock.

A classroom of average size.
Tables and chairs scattered about.
Tables isolated against a wall.

"Maybe you want some time alone."

Rugs on which to sit. Rugs on which to lie.
Corners in which to put your shoes.
My rocking chair.

Games, puzzles, records, building tools, building blocks,
wood,
trucks,
easels and paint.
The walls are bare when first you come.
Here is a folder.
You may decorate it if you wish.
Then, pin it on the waiting wall.
There is your name for all to see.
You exist for me.
But how do you exist for you?
You say, "I'll beat him up; then he'll know who I am."
Anger.
Anger.
That is real for you.

But anger is not usually acceptable in school.
You play "bully."
You play "helpless."
You say,

> **"I won't."**
> **"I can't."**
> **"You can't make me."**
> **"You're not my mama."**

Steve, you walk in an hour late.
Norma, you won't talk.
You respond to "a school."
You respond to "a schoolroom."
You respond to "a teacher."

> **"I won't."**
> **"I can't."**

Each of you carries your own expectation. Each of you has his own image. Each of you tries to avoid what is happening "now."

Reggie, you fling open the door, stomp in, look around, go over to Steven and you hit him.

"What are you doing, Reggie?"

"Nothing."

"What did you just do to Steven?"

"Steven looked at me."

"What did *you* do to Steven?"

"Steven's a baby."

"What did you do to Steven?"

"Hit him." (You are smiling slightly.)

"Yes, now put that into a sentence starting with the word 'I.' "

"I hit Steven." (Your slight smile is now a big smile.)

I have introduced you to the "now." I am also building your awareness, Reggie. I am trying to make you aware of what *you* are doing. I am trying to make you aware of your existence. I will continue with this process, for you will not accept awareness easily.

"What are you doing now, Reggie?"

> **"Now I am hitting Norma."**
> **"Now I am yelling at you."**
> **"Now I am learning to write."**
> **"Now I am hugging you."**

Reggie, I will try to make you aware of your existence every time you write a story or paint a picture. I will try to make you aware of your existence by having you look into a mirror. And, Reggie, I have a Polaroid camera ready when you do something you thought impossible.

"What are you doing now, Reggie?"

> **"Sawing a piece of wood for my boat."**

"Who is sawing the wood?"

"I am sawing a piece of wood for my boat."

"How are you working?"

"Quietly and not bothering anyone else."

"Who is working quietly and not bothering anyone else?"

"I am working quietly and not bothering anyone else."

"Have a piece of candy, Reggie."

Richard, you walk into the room
Body rigid
Face frowning.
You talk with no one.
You look around. You see Kenny.

"You're a baby!"

Kenny answers,

"I can beat you up."

Richard,

"You need your cousin Larry to help you!"

Kenny,

"You need your whole generation!"

You both begin to circle around each other. I take your fight seriously. I keep the other children quiet. I watch you. You know I am watching you. Richard, you pick up a wooden block.

"You may fight. But you must fight with only your hands. Put down the wooden block."

You put down the block. You accept the rule.

*C*hests high
Shoulders back
Circle
Circle
Push with your chests
Push with your shoulders
Eye to eye
Circle round
Round the room
Circle round
Around each other
Your fight is a ritual
Your fight is a dance.

You strike at each other. I watch. I will not allow either of you to be injured. You stop and you circle again. You make contact with your body, your anger, your aggression. You circle. You exchange blows. You scuffle.

From time to time you make sure that I am watching. The encounter begins to lose steam. You are circling the room. You are not touching anymore.

Words,

> **"I don't want to beat you up today."**
> **"I could beat you up if I wanted to."**

Your movements are slowing down.
I ask,

> **"Are you finished?"**

You answer,

> **"Not yet."**

You circle awhile longer.
Your energy is spent.

"Richard, what do you want to do now?"

"I want to play with the blocks."

"Go ahead."

"Kenny, what do you want to do now?"

"I want to play with the blocks."

"Go ask Richard if you can play with him."

Kenny, you are willing to ask Richard. Richard, you say yes. You both join together to build a very complex structure. You have learned another way of contacting one another. With your arms around each other you run up to me.

"Come look at what we built!"

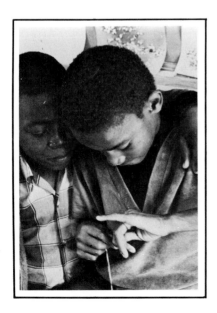

G*ames and puzzles;*
dolls and trucks scattered about the room.
Pencils on the floor . . . spilled paint.

> **"I want to write. I can't find a stupid pencil."**
> **"I want to paint. I can't find a fucking brush."**
> **"Give me a pencil."**
> **"Find me a brush."**
> **"Buy some new puzzles."**
> **"Get some new trucks."**
> **"Buy me . . ."**
> **"Give me . . ."**
> **"Fuck you . . . this is a fucking room."**
> **"I am going to steal a ball from another room."**

I am not here to "pick up" after you. I am not here to take care of the tools you use, or the games you enjoy. If I "pick up" after you, you will not experience the frustration of missing parts and broken toys. If I take care of your things you will have no way of discovering how to care for your equipment. I will do nothing for you that you are capable of doing for yourself.

We gather at the rocking chair. There you encounter the toys, games and equipment. You encounter the room. You explore and discover new ways of responding to school.

After repeated frustration and repeated work together you begin to say,

> **"I'm going to clean up now."**
> **"Don't let Troy play with the games . . . he breaks everything."**

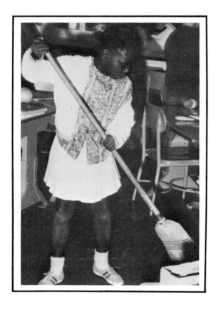

Children, you live in a chaotic world. Your world can expand beyond your chaos. The first step in this process is for you to touch your chaos. You must touch your chaos; you must live through your chaotic experiences in the classroom. You must not avoid these experiences. So often the super-structure of school does not permit this kind of contact. Here and now you are free; you are free to come into contact with your chaos.

"Rearrange the room."

Moving furniture.
Tables pushed . . . pulled.
Chairs sliding across the room.
Noise mounting.
I watch.
Random movement.
An hour passes . . . no order, no direction.
Random motion.
The motion slows.
The furniture still chaotic.
You are walking, moving, no direction.
No direction.
No order.
Soon you avoid touching the furniture.
Soon you avoid looking at each other.
Random contact.
Noise.

"This room looks dumb."
"I don't want to be in this room."

Silent room.
Children, you begin to look at me.
You are beginning to touch your immobility.
You are beginning to be in touch with your need for help.
I wait.
I will not respond to you until you make an explicit demand for my help.

Soon you say,

"I don't know what to do."
"Where can I put this table?"

I suggest that you put four tables in the center of the room.
You want help . . . you accept help.
The movement takes on direction.

In the process of doing, you discover that you have ideas of your own. As the semester continues, you learn to suggest changes periodically. You try various arrangements. You begin to get in touch with "change."

You are children, children who still need your mothers. You protect your mothers.

"Nobody calls my mother a name."

Troy, you walk into the room, you look at me, and you yell,

"You don't do anything right, you black bitch!"

We all gather in a circle at the rocking chair. I start talking about getting angry at the people with whom we live.

"How do some of the people you live with make you angry?"

"My brother tears my books."
"My father whips me."

Soon Troy, you say,

"My mother didn't cook my hamburger enough."

I ask you to come sit next to me. You walk over and sit down. You have a frown on your face. There is an empty chair in front of you.

"Troy, pretend your mother is sitting in that empty chair in front of you. Tell her what you are angry about. You may say anything you want to say, since she is not really here."

Troy, you begin,

"Mama, you know this meat is raw. I hate raw meat."

Troy, sit in the other chair and pretend to be your mother. What does she say?

"I didn't know it was raw."

"Now be Troy again."

"Mama, you don't do anything right!"

"Now be your mother."

"I wash your clothes. I iron your shirts so you'll look good for school."

"Now be Troy again."

"I know. But I can't eat this hamburger. I'm going to throw it away and make another one."

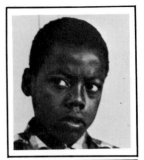

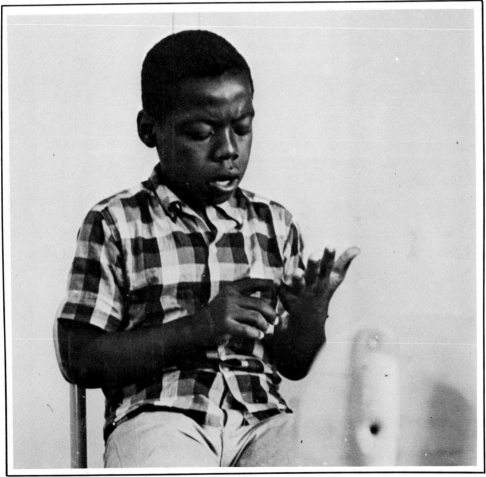

You continue with this dialogue. You tell your mother what you resent and also you tell her what you appreciate. Your mother is not destroyed. Next, you begin to expand your world; instead of throwing the hamburger away, you discover other "possible" solutions for the situation.

"Troy, look at the children in the room; look at me. What do you see? Is there anyone here you are angry with?"

You look around the room, you smile, you become somewhat shy. You are aware of yourself; you are aware of others. Your anger is finished. You can see us.

Troy, you answer,

> **"No, I'm not mad at anybody. Can I take the ball out at recess?"**

Patrick, you run into the room yelling,

> **"She took away our ball. That Mrs. Brown is a bitch. I didn't do anything."**

I suggest you come up to the chair next to me; put Mrs. Brown in the empty chair and tell her what you are angry about. When you start to play the "blaming game," I suggest you bring the situation into the "now" and have an encounter with whomever you are blaming. Depending on what you can accept, I either stop you with the awareness of both sides of the situation or you go on to explore other possible ways of behavior which may be more appropriate to the situation.

"I won't!"
"I can't!"
"I don't want to read that dumb book!"

Books are of little value to you as they do not relate to your present world.

"I hate my fucking sister. She beat me up!"

You have just told an explicit story with words that have explicit meaning for you. I suggest that you write your story.

"I don't know how to spell the words."

I write the words on a separate piece of paper and you write them on your paper. I give you the words as you ask for them. This is also proof that I am listening to you. If you are ready, the same story can be expanded into fantasy. You may find other emotions available to you. As a result, your real world may expand.

"What would you like to do to your sister?"

"I can't do anything. She is bigger than I am."

"She is not here and this is just pretend. Tell her what you would like to do to her."

"I'd like to hit you."

"What else would you like to do?"

"I'd like to kick you."

"What else?"

"That's all, I'm finished."

Now you begin to write your story. You are full of energy. You are completing unfinished business.

You read your story back to me. You can now read it to anyone you choose. You pin your story on the wall. You put it above your name. Your emotions exist and you are acceptable. You are real and you are real to others. You have made another contact with your expanding world.

The above is a process, not a task, in which reading and writing become an integral and creative way for you to relate to your world. The process deals with *your* fears, your fantasies, your various personae, your mother, father, siblings, cousins, teachers, and neighbors and not with "Dick and Jane and the Fireman," who are nothing to you.

"I won't."
"I can't."
"Maybe I can."

The name of this game is "Get the Middle-class Teacher's Goat!"
You wait for the room to be very quiet. You begin to sing when
you see another child who you imagine will sing along with you. It is
even better if there are two or three who seem to be possible joiners.
You select a very special song.

> **"I have a girl from Culver City,**
> **She's got meat balls on her titties.**
> **She's got ham and eggs**
> **Between her legs . . ."**

I listen. You repeat your song.

"I like the way you boys sing. Come over to the tape recorder."

We all walk over to the tape recorder. I suggest you sing your song
into the tape recorder. Your eyes are getting very big.

> **"Oh no! You're going to take it to the principal."**

"I like the way you sing. You can erase the tape when we are
finished."

You begin to giggle. You are willing to take the risk. The tape
recorder intrigues you. You begin to sing. I play the tape right back.
You listen. You laugh.

> **"My voice sounds funny."**
> **"That's no good. You could hear us laughing."**
> **"Let's do it again."**

You sing again. This time there is more concern with the sound and the rhythm. You listen again. You are beginning to like your voices. You begin to improvise; you pick up something to drum. We have another taping session.

"Hey, I know a better song."

You rearrange your positions for greater quality. Your rhythm is becoming more complex. You listen again.

"Hey, man, I sound good."
"Hey, we could go on T.V."
"Hey, could we sing for the school?"

The game is over. Each of you has discovered another part of yourself. Another way to relate to your world. I have not fulfilled your expectations of anger, shock and punishment. I avoided a frontal attack on "meat balls and titties."

"I can sing."
"I can listen to me."
"Listen to me."
"Look at me."

"I want."
"I want you to see me."
"I want to *know* that you see me."

Your day begins long before you arrive at school. Billy, you prepared your own breakfast. Mike, you packed your own lunch. Ricky, you have taken care of youngers brothers and sisters. Jenny, you have washed dishes and ironed clothes. Some of you will go home to make your own dinners. Some of you will go to homes where the adults have left for work, or are returning . . . tired and frustrated.

You come to school.
Some of the adults here at school say you are irresponsible.

Bobby, your mother is very tired. She works hard at the hospital. She is not sure of how to help you with your schoolwork. Her own experience at school was not pleasant. Joe, your mother feels alone; there is no one to give to her. She loves you . . . she wants to help you . . . she tries to give you attention . . . she also needs attention. Geraldine, your mother has many other children to care for and so you must share what little energy she has.

Here at school I will attempt to give you immediate attention. You need attention now . . . you do not need to learn to wait. You know about waiting and waiting and waiting. You are hungry now!

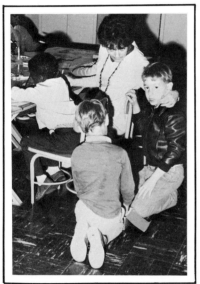

Robert, you just wrote your first story. I give you a piece of candy. I give you attention *now*. I give you another piece of candy after you read your story for me. Gradually I will change the candy into points that you can save and exchange for toys. That will happen when you are ready. You are very pleased about your story.

"Robert, take your story and show it to the principal. Ask him to sign his name on it."

You go to his office . . . you read your story. He praises you. You run into the room smiling. You show me where he signed your paper . . . more concrete proof for you of your existence and proof of your ability to do what you thought impossible.

"Robert, go read your paper to Mrs. McCambell, our custodian. She has known you for a long time. Have her sign your paper."

Once again you run out of the room. You return smiling. You are having fun boasting about your new academic achievement! I give you another point.

"I want to go read my story to Mrs. Jones. She was my teacher last year."

With a new confidence about yourself, off you *run!* There is no point in asking you to walk.

You return and staple your story on the wall over your name.
You work with numbers.
You want to practise your printing.
You want to write another story.
Today there is no stopping you!
Tomorrow you may play with blocks all day, you may do nothing, you may need to prove that you can still be a "bully."
Achieving the impossible can be scary the first time.
I will not push you.

"Robert, do you want a ride home?"

"Yes."

We walk out to my car together.

"My teacher is going to drive me home."

We drive up to your apartment house. Many children are playing. "Go tell your mother I am here and ask her if it is all right for me to come in."

I see your mother.
She is tired.
She is deeply tired.
She becomes defensive and angry, assuming I am there to
report your misbehavior. *Her* anger is real. I show her
your work. Her face changes. I see her smile.

> **"I knew you could do this kind of work, Robert. I knew it all
> the time."**

Robert, your married sister lives in the apartment above yours. Your
mother says,

> **"Go get your sister. Tell her to come down and meet your
> teacher and see your schoolwork."**

I experience your mother's warmth. I experience her relief.
You experience her warmth. You experience her attention.
You run upstairs and get your sister.
You both return.
You become shy.
We are all in touch with each other.
We are all a little shy.
You are still in touch with your new self-confidence.

> **"Mama, I am going to earn a toy next week!"**

I am
I can.

I CAN . . .

I can listen

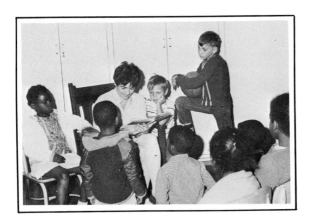

I can write

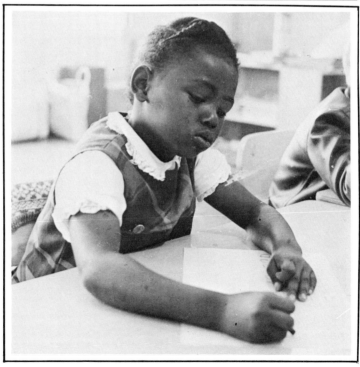

I can work

I can build

"I am."
"I can see me."
"I can see you."

You begin to relate with me.
I do not meet your expectations of
      "a teacher."
You begin to call me,
      "Miss Lederman"
      or
      "Miss Litterbug,"
      or
      "Janet."
You are beginning to see *me*. For so long you called me "teacher."

I provide you with the opportunity to see other adults. Adults are all different. We have different things available for you. Children, you are different and have different needs at different times. I cannot fill *all* your demands . . . all your needs.

The volunteer, adults who join our classroom one or two days each week, each one has something available for you.

Some of them will play games with you, some of them will be available to sit next to you while you write a story or do arithmetic. Some will bring music experiences for you. Some will bring craft experiences for you. Some will play ball with you, some will just listen to you. The "other adults" . . . they can give you some of the immediate attention you need. These men and women of the larger community are available to you and now you are available to them. I give no formal instruction on how you "should" relate with each other. You will both have to find your own level of communication. The volunteers who don't find a way will leave . . . those who do find a way stay on and children, you use them . . . you relate to them and you learn from many sources.

Mrs. L. brings her accordion and a rich background in music. She brings her guitar and whistles and musical games.

"I want to work with Mrs. L. today!"
"I want to play the accordion!"
"I want to learn to read music!"
"I want to learn to sing in French!"

"Go ask Mrs. L. how many children she can work with at one time."

Sometimes so many want to work with Mrs. L. you have to take turns. Sometimes just a few of you want to work. Sometimes only one of you wants to work and you work for as long as you are interested.

Mrs. C. brings reading games and word games and special puzzles.

> **"Here comes Mrs. C. Can I go help her carry her things into the room?"**
> **"I want to read with Mrs. C. first!"**
> **"I am going to work with her all day!"**

Mrs. S. is available to help you with stories and arithmetic. She doesn't like doing puzzles. Mrs. S. is an old friend. She has been part of our classroom for two years. Mrs. G. loves to work on puzzles and she likes to go on the yard and play ball. You take what is available from each one. You learn about them and they learn about you. You begin to trust more and more.

I become less important.

"I can stay in school all day."
"I can read."
"I can."
"I am."

Your world is expanding. You begin to see other rooms. They seem available for you now.

"I want to go to Miss Oshrin's room."

"Go ask Miss Oshrin if you can visit her room today."

"You ask her."

"I don't want to go to Miss Oshrin's room."

"O.K., then write me a note."

"You don't need a note from me. You go ask *her* for a note saying it is all right for you to visit today."

"I am afraid to go ask her."

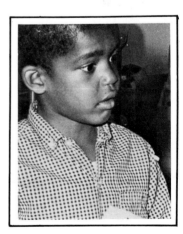

"Then stay here." I walk away.

"I'm going to Miss Oshrin's room."

Smiling, you leave the room.

You are willing to take a risk. You visit, you stay for a short while. *You* know when you are ready to come back. You try other rooms. You come back. You are very selective. You begin to explore more and more. I begin to accommodate your needs less and less. You are beginning to get in touch with boredom here in this room. You know a little about what is available to you in other situations. Your exploration continues. You begin to feel your strengths. You have successes. You experience failure, you are able to accept some failure now. *You* are not a failure.

> **"Look at the story I wrote in Miss Carney's room today."**
> **"I did spelling in Miss Cutler's room."**
> **"Mr. Cardinal says I have to read this book before I can build a boat in his room. Help me learn to read it."**

Dancing, moving

You have fun being animals sleeping
finding food
fighting

You have fun discovering the ways in which your body can move
human fingers move this way
paws move that way

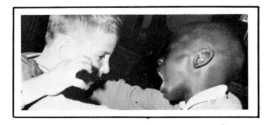

You have fun being snakes and lizards sliding and slipping
You have fun being birds and making your arms into wings
I watch you when you are tigers and listen to you roar
I hear you pounding drums

I see you plucking the strings of a guitar
You use your left hand, then your right
You use your hand, your head, your foot to make a balloon go across
the room
I hear your laughter as you run with your kite.

I hear you scream with delight.
Feather dusters moved by your hands to your own rhythms, inside
and out.
You run to me and give me a hug.
I see you,
I feel you, we touch each other's worlds.

EPILOGUE

Dear Reader,

I cannot write an epilogue. There is no conclusion to education, there is only a process, and the process has no conclusion.

A process of emerging education.
An experimental approach to learning.
The integration of the "I" and the "educator."
The "I" as the creator, I, creating an environment for discovery.
The when, where, and how of learning.
Cooperative living . . . The child and the adult.
I and Thou.
The poetry of self.
My own rhythm.
Resting.
Flowing.
The heat of energy awakening the dormant "I."
I am flowing, I am dancing. I am singing, I am crying.
Together and apart.
The flow of in and out contracting and expanding.
One generation flowing into the other.
Getting through the impasse, transcending the status quo.

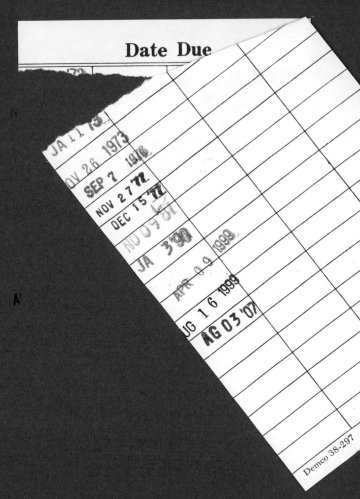